What Happened to the Playbook?

From the Newark Streets to the NFL
…and the Long Road Back

by Reggie "Truck" Brown

Contributing author Leontyne H. Anglin. Staging Executives.

ISBN-13: 978-1546812265
ISBN-10: 1546812261

PRE-GAME

"I left New Jersey in 1978 with a one-way ticket, $50, and a suitcase and I said I'm not coming back until I make something of myself and become somebody.

I didn't do it alone.

This book is dedicated to all of those who cared and helped me along the way.

First, I would like to take a moment to thank my Lord and Savior Jesus Christ who makes it all possible in my life every single time that I wake up to see another day.

Thank you Londa Murphy Brown for the two most precious gifts Reggie (RD) and Rabia (Bia). To my family Pam, Donnell, Carl, Treasy, Terrie, Shareise and Louie. I love all of you.

My two best friends Craig McCoy and Vincson Green. I truly appreciate your support. You're the best.

To my Bull("Dogs") Haasan, Kevin, and Rick. Thanks for being there no matter what.

To my Shabazz High School Bulldog coaches Mr. Finch, Mr. Reynolds, Mr. Bulger and Mr. Ed Peart, you all taught me how to be a man. Thank you.

To my Bulldog mentors Lamont Merritt, Maxwell White, Barry Pryor, Todd Fleming, Malcolm Jones, Rhino Rob, and James Walker. Thanks for showing me the way.

To my Pasadena City College Coaches Harvey Hyde and Eric Widmark thanks for giving me the opportunity. You changed my life, forever.

Thanks Dr. Lee for mentoring and keeping me together through all my sports injuries.

To Jeannie and the Simmons family thanks for never giving up on me.

To my Oregon Connection - the Green family and the Gilbert family, because of all of you I never went hungry.

Sending thanks to my Kappa Alpha Psi Fraternity family, Legal Shield family, Agape family, Pentecostal Church of Christ family and of course The Rooms.

To Terri Sampson thank you for supporting me through thick and thin. So much I can say about you. Thank you and your family. Love you.

To my friend Leontyne Anglin, thanks for your continued support and encouraging dialogue over the years and keeping me on point. I owe you everything. You truly are the best.

I know that I may have missed some but please blame my head and not my heart.

To Mom and Dad, your love was all that I ever needed.

Thank you always."

Dendron, Virginia

CONTENTS

1 PRE-GAME – Dedication iii

2 1st QUARTER – Newark Streets Page 10

3 2nd QUARTER – College Daze Page 20

4 3rd QUARTER – The Pros Page 50

5 4th QUARTER – Life After Football Page 71

6 POST-GAME – NFL Pro to CEO Page 84

Sometimes you have to be blatantly honest.

Most people think you just put on a football uniform and make a million dollars. They see the glitz and glamour of the lifestyle during the game but those lifestyle changes you have to make afterwards, that's a whole different ball game.

I can't hide behind the truth.

You know what I really learned in college? I mastered how to be an alcoholic and a drug addict. In return, they gave me a reward.

A diploma. A piece of paper with my name on it.

The night before my wedding, I was getting blasted. I started the whole thing off on the wrong foot. When I was at my worst, I realized that the best thing I could have done at that time was to leave. I didn't lose my family. I gave up my family.

No one twisted my arm or held a gun to my head for the choices that I made. This book is about what can happen to your life when there's no more team. No more guidance. No more structure ... No more playbook.

I've been carrying this around in my spirit for too long. Someone needs to hear it.

Let's go!

1ST
QUARTER
" BROWN

An exclusive interview with Reggie "Truck" Brown

Interviewer**:** Thanks for taking your time to share this exclusive interview. Let's just jump right in Reggie. The title of this book is "*What Happened to the Playbook*?" So where did the journey begin for you?

Reggie**:** I was born in Dendron, Virginia but came up in Newark, New Jersey. For as long as I could remember, I wanted to play football but coming from a large family we didn't have the money for Pop Warner or anything like that. So we played street ball.

That's where it all started. On the Newark streets. We played against each other representing the street that we lived on.

I lived on Bergen Street, so the name of my team was the Bergen Street Blue Bombers. We played against teams like the Hillside Cowboys and the Hunterdon Fingerprints. They had fingerprints on the side of their helmets. We played the Peshine Undertakers. They were the dirty bunch. They would kill you for real! (laughter).

I'm thankful for my loving parents. My mom was always there through thick and thin no matter what. My dad was there too. You know, he was an athlete but didn't get a chance to play in the pros or even college. He made it to the 11th grade but I can tell you he was my greatest hero.

That was my life being a kid. You always want to try and hold on to that childlike spirit because when you lose that, you lose a lot.

But, sometimes you grow up fast.

My dad was my hero and he also gave me my first joint. He didn't know what he was doing. But that one joint led me to cocaine and cocaine led to the alcohol. One thing led to another and eventually it started catching up with me.

So by the time I entered the NFL and had the money to get whatever I wanted, that's what started the downward spiral.

Most people think it's all glitz and glamour when you make it to the NFL. You make a whole bunch of money and you live like a king.

But no one ever thinks about what really goes on behind the scenes.

Let me tell you. I've been through it all. You name it, I did it. From the drugs, the alcohol, the sex, the whole nine. Most people never want to talk about that.

The reality is most of my life I've been dealing with a playbook starting from my days at Shabazz High School. I was a good player but I didn't always listen. I guess you could say that I didn't have a lot of discipline. I pretty much did what I wanted to do.

It wasn't until one of my coaches kicked me in the butt, literally, and sat me on the bench that I started to pay attention. It was the first steps that started to put me on the right path. The path that would ultimately help lead me from Newark out into a world that I may otherwise have never known.

Most of my friends that I hung out with for so many years who will read this are gonna' ask Reggie, you really did that? Well yeah, I did.

And believe me I never did anything half way. I did them the whole way. I've slowed down a little bit. The reason I slowed down is because there's a new challenge today. I want to help more people because of where I've been.

> *Today I believe that if you help enough people get what they want, you'll get yours by default.*

Looking back, there were so many good times and lessons learned during my high school years. The friends on and off the field, the coaches who kicked me in the butt. It was all a learning ground.

***Interviewer*:** So, if you had to sum it up and say one of the biggest lessons you learned in your first quarter … what do you think that was?

Reggie: Things are not always as they appear, and if you don't listen you sure can't learn. And… if you don't want that foot to come, do what you're told.

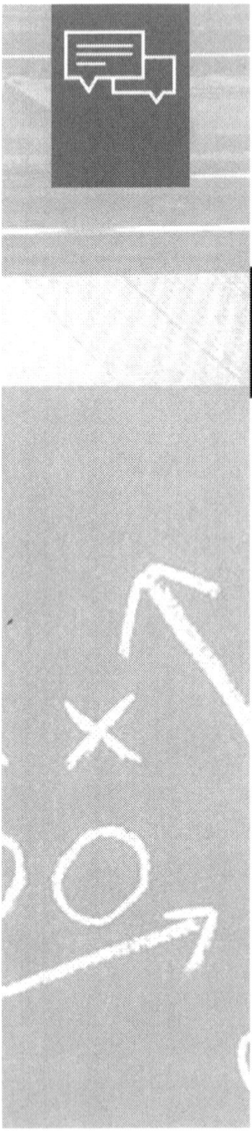

CREATE YOUR OWN PLAYBOOK.

What hobbies did you enjoy in your early years?

Hobbies:

Potential opportunities:

Example: teaching a workshop, starting a business, applying to college or certificate program

2ND
QUARTER

***Interviewer*:** So, you made it through and learned some valuable lessons in high school. What about college? Do you feel like college prepared you for what you were going to face in the pros?

***Reggie*:** College life was definitely something that I needed because I don't think you can really prepare for the pros without going to college. I know for me going from Newark, New Jersey to California and then to Oregon, that was a journey all by itself.

I had to follow the rules and regulations and follow the plan that was given to me. So that playbook was definitely self-imposed.

I'm 3,000 miles away from home. I can't say Mom, I'm in trouble come help me out or Dad come get me. I started to realize that I needed to take this opportunity seriously. Especially Oregon - it was like a different world altogether.

New surroundings and new sights to see right in front of me and I experimented with just about everything. To this day, I'm thankful for my coaches, mentors and families that took me in to make sure I was okay.

Someone asked me once why do you think they put lines in the road? Well to keep you from killing yourself that's pretty much what it is but it's really to keep you in line. Because if you get out of line, you will definitely hurt yourself.

Interviewer: When did you start to realize that you were good enough to head to college level football?

Reggie: I think it was my junior year of high school when I started making a little bit of noise. But I hurt my back in my senior year and they told me I wouldn't able to play sports again for the rest of my life. I ended up wearing a brace on my back that last year but did play in a few games.

Only 4 schools were interested in me coming. One of them was Syracuse but when they found out my grade point average was 1.99, it wasn't good enough. Another was Northeastern up in Boston. They didn't care what my grades were so I kind of didn't want to go there.

So I ended up going to a Pasadena City College – a junior college out in California. When I got started there, I was #7 on the depth chart.

Things were starting to happen in my first year. I played Fullback, Tailback and shared duties with a lot of people. I got a chance to play when someone got hurt and if we won this game, we would end up going to a Bowl game. It was the last game of the season. I was playing Tailback the whole game – ended up running 145 yards, scored a touchdown and we won. We later went on to play in the Potato Bowl. I ran for 277 yards and scored 4 touchdowns!

Interviewer: Did your grades get any better while you were in junior college?

Reggie: Yes, I had a chance to focus on some things that I didn't do in high school and started to concentrate on why I was there. A lot of people say they went to school to get a degree. I'm going tell the truth …

I went to school to play football!

By my 2nd year, my grades improved to like a 2.3 or 2.4. It wasn't a whole lot better, but it was better than what it was before. I realized that while I was in school that I needed to focus on the books because bottom line is -- nobody wants a dummy.

Interviewer: So, at the end of your 2nd year Oregon started looking at you. How did they get into the picture and what were they looking for?

Reggie: Well by this point, I had become a Junior College All American. I ran for 1,549 yards scored 16 touchdowns and we had played in the Bowl game. By that time, I had all the colleges around the country that wanted me to come play for them. Florida State, Oklahoma, LSU, Southern Cal, UCLA, everybody. Turns out my head coach at Pasadena became the Offensive Coordinator at the University of Oregon. He knew what I did and I knew what kind of offense he ran so it was good fit. Like I said, I had the chance to go anywhere around the country, but went to Oregon because if was different.

As I said, it was an experience for me. Nothing like I've seen before. In Newark, there was all sidewalks and no trees. In Oregon, it was no sidewalks and all trees. Listen, I was white water rafting and doing all kinds of things just having a great time. I went to tutors in the morning, then to class and then to tutors again in the afternoon. They made sure we did those things.

Interviewer: There are many parents out there and their kids want to play collegiate football, what are the scouts looking for at the college level?

Reggie: They're looking for mature young men with a great attitude. You can be a great football player with a bad attitude – they don't want that. Back in my day, football players were a dime a dozen. You could be good player, didn't think a lot and didn't do well in school but they played you anyway. Now, times have changed. If you're not taking care of the books, they don't want you. If you have a bad attitude, they don't want you.

Interviewer: Do they look at the grades?

Reggie: If you have the potential to be a great student then you have an opportunity to be a great football player. You know, football players are made so if you can combine the talent with the grades you can have a whole new level of opportunities.

I'm going to tell you though for me it took me 15 years after I finished playing ball to get my degree because I couldn't get past Algebra. I just couldn't grasp it even with going to tutors before and after class but I put in the effort. I was there. I showed up and did everything that I could. They eventually passed me when I took the class Pass/Fail but I believe it's because I was there and put forth all my effort to do the best that I could.

Interviewer: I see. So now you're at Oregon, when do you start thinking hey I might be able to go to the NFL?

Reggie: Well you know ever since I was knee high to a duck I wanted to play pro ball. I was a little guy and remember this one Christmas me and my two brothers got football uniforms. They came in a little box – the whole thing, helmet, shoulder pads, pants, and the jersey. We put it on and went down to the sand lot and played football. It was COLD – we were freezing!

My favorite team then was the Baltimore Colts. I saw a game and all these people were hollering screaming the name of the players when they scored touchdowns and I said I want some of that.

So while I'm in Oregon, I had an opportunity to see this thing happen right in front of me. You're talking tens of thousands of people yelling when you scored a touchdown. I wanted that. You know, we had a pretty good ball club. We played in the PAC10 with lots of talented guys going to the pros.

I kept doing what I was supposed to be doing, kept my head in the books and stayed in the classroom preparing for my chance to come one day.

Interviewer: Now you're really into the world of college football, what are some of the things you can remember about the process throughout the whole year?

Reggie: Well football season is a whole year long thing. Ball players are much bigger, stronger and faster because they're training differently. I'm not sure what they're eating or what they're feeding these guys today but I was watching a game the other night, the guy was like 6'7, 300 pounds and could run like a deer! If he was chasing me man, I don't run like that. That's how they're being groomed now so training is something that you do all year long.

During high school, we basically practiced during football season. But when you get to college you have spring ball. You have to get ready for that with a little time off in the summer. When you come back from the summer break you must be ready because the season is going to start. I tell you I don't care how good a ball player you are, you have to concentrate on being a good student because they'll let you go. From the college perspective, if you're not taking care of the books, you can't help them.

Interviewer: So how does it work with scholarships to get onto a team?

Reggie: Well for me when I came out of high school and headed to Pasadena, it wasn't necessarily on scholarships it was more grants plus work study through a job that I had on campus. But the time I got to Oregon, I was on a full scholarship. They paid for everything. I couldn't have a job then. I really couldn't do anything. You know it was pretty hard because you see some students driving nice cars. Well I had a bike. At the end of the day though, I never went hungry and I always had food in my freezer. The coaches really looked out for me.

To this day, I still have an associate from the college 35 years later. This guy still calls me and says Hey Reggie, I love you. He calls me all the time. There were people that truly cared about the student athletes. I'm thankful for people that I met that are still in my life because I went to school for the football scholarship but made some friends along the way and it made me a better person and taught me some things in life.

Brown is Lancers' new secret weapon

By ROGER MURRAY
Staff Writer

It was a clear day indeed.

The San Gabriel Mountains were easily visible to the North, thanks to the Santa Anas which had blown away the usually present grey-brown atmosphere in which Valley residents normally reside. Reggie Brown sat on the top steps of the football stadium at Pasadena City College and gazed eastward. Still, he was neither high enough nor was the air clear enough for him to find what he was looking for.

"I'd sure like to see my home," he said, smiling as he thought about friends and family. "But that's a long way off, and it'll be a while, probably not till Christmas, before I see any of those people."

Brown is a fullback for PCC's Metropolitan Conference defending champions. He also is from Shabazz High School in Newark, N.J.

A 208-pound freshman who ran the 100 in 9.9 in high school, Brown has joined with sophomore Mike McLellan to give the Lancers perhaps their most productive position, in terms of execution.

In Saturday night's stirring, come-from-behind, 27-22 Metro win over East Los Angeles College, Brown gained 32 yards in five carries, and hauled in a 13-yard touchdown pass that pulled his club to within two points during the third quarter.

A week ago, in the Metro opener against Bakersfield, Brown surprised the Renegades with his speed by flashing 57 yards down the sideline for a touchdown, and through four games (he missed the first two with a hip pointer) he is averaging just under eight yards a carry for 20 rushes. He's also caught five passes for 50 yards.

ELAC). They are doing all we could ask of them."

For McLellan, it may be a bit more comfortable because as a former all-Pacific Leaguer from Arcadia High School, he's playing in his back yard. For Brown, it can be a lonely existence at times.

"I worked and saved my money this summer to get out here, and I'm happy I made the move," he said. "But some times it does get lonely. I miss my family and the people I grew up with. It's natural to want to play before people you know."

Brown admits playing football has a lot to do with his life. It means staying in school, and hopefully making it easier to go to a bigger four-year institution four years from now.

"If it weren't for football, I'm not sure what I'd be doing," he explains. "Maybe I'd be in the army. It's not what I want, but maybe that would be my only other choice.

"The area I grew up in wasn't all that bad, but it wasn't exactly the best either, and a lot of the guys spent their time just hanging out on the street. I decided early that wasn't for me, that it led in the wrong direction.

"It was easy to see that sports in general and football in particular was the best way for me."

Without any offers from major universities, Brown decided the best bet was a junior college. He found his way to Pasadena through a chain of coaches who recommended Wismark and PCC.

"It's probably one of the best known junior colleges in the country, certainly in our area, so I made up my mind to come here for two years," said the likeable, well-mannered Brown.

"I'd like to get home for Thanksgiving, but financially it looks like it will be an either-or — either Thanksgiving or Christmas. We'll still be involved in football at Thanksgiving, and I'll have a little more time at Christmas, so I guess that's it."

Brown looked to the east again.

"I like it out here a lot," he said softly, "and the people have really been good to me. But it's still not quite home, and it sure would be nice...."

Reggie Brown on the move

Reggie Brown-277 yards on 13 carries

MOST VALUABLE—Freshman tailback Reggie Brown (48) rushed 35 times for 277 yards and four the game's Most Valuable Player honors. In the fourth quarter alone, he tallied 146 yards on 13

EN ROUTE TO RECORD — College of Sequoias' Eric Shannon (16) thinks he's going to stop Pasadena City College tailback Reggie Brown (48) as this sweep develops, but Brown ran right through Shannon's tackle to gain nine yards. With teammates like David Jines (65) opening the holes for him, Brown rushed for 277 yards and four TDs, both records, in PCC's 31-28 win in Saturday night's Potato Bowl in Bakersfield. Brown was named the game's Most Valuable Player.

PCC win: Potato Bowl's 'best game since 1952'

By ROGER MURRAY
Staff Writer

Pasadena City College had just beaten College of Sequoias, 31-28, in a thrilling, come-from-behind decision, and as he walked out of Bakersfield's Memorial Stadium, one veteran observer remarked, "That's the best bowl game they've had here since Bakersfield beat Fresno (25-19) in '52."

It just might have been.

The Lancers, 7-3 and Metropolitan Conference champions for the second straight year, were underdogs against a sophomore-laden COS team that won 8 of 10 games and captured the Valley Conference title with a 5-1 mark.

A year ago, PCC defeated COS, 24-21, in a come-from-behind thriller en route to Jr. Rose Bowl and National championships. Just as in 1952 when the lead changed hands four times and wasn't decided until the final gun, Saturday night's cold and windy clash before 8,337 fans featured a see-saw change of leader and a fourth-quarter comeback by the winners that [illegible]

on which he broke three tackles within 15 yards of the line of scrimmage.

He was selected the game's Most Valuable Player, joining teammate Mitchell Pounds as an individual award winner.

Pounds, a 6-3, 260-pound sophomore from Blair High School, was named the game's Outstanding Defensive Player after making eight primary tackles and assisting on six others.

COS tailback Darryl Minor, who gained 189 yards in 33 carries before leaving the game with an ankle injury at the end of the third quarter, received the Outstanding Offensive Player award.

After playing turnover-free ball in a pair of pressure-packed games at the regular season's end, Pasadena made two of them against COS that quickly were converted into 14 points.

PCC tailback David Baxter fumbled at the end of a 13-yard gain on the third play of the game and Ben Rudolph recovered for the Giants.

Nine plays later, with Minor doing most of the work, including

out, again behind the strong blocks of Wehnert and McLellan.

COS came right back with a sustained, 14-play, 80-yard march with Miller crashing over from 1-yard away to tie the count at 14-14. The Giants regained the lead near the end of the first half as Pat Lais intercepted Murray's pass over the middle at the PCC 44, and four plays later, Miller again scored from one yard out. Quarterback Bob Daniels hit Darren Long for a 37-yard gain to set up the score.

The Giants appeared as though they would end their two-game losing streak in the Potato Bowl

Turn to LANCERS,
Page B-4, this section

LANCER BOOTY — This is just some of the hardware picked up by Pasadena City College's football program over the past two years. Shown are the 1977 and 1978 Potato Bowl trophies and this year's Potato Bowl Most Valuable Player trophy awarded to Lancer running back Reggie Brown. PCC has won 19 of 22 games over the past two years and in a recent poll came out with the top-ranked JC football program in the country over the past 11 years.

Lancer grid program more than just playing football

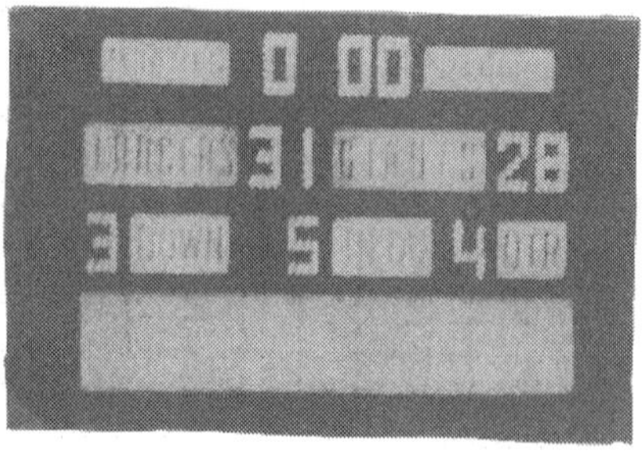

Potato Bowl Most Valuable Player Reggie Brown

PCC wins Metro grid title...

Continued from Page C-1

called back to Murray, who then threw to wide receiver Chuck Allen, who had been streaking down the sideline. Allen caught the ball, put a move on a Brahma defender at the 15 and raced into the end zone to complete the 57-yard play. Doug Jollymour kicked the point-after for a 7-0 lead with 4:15 left in the first quarter.

Jollymour added a 16-yard field goal with 1:11 left in the same period for a 10-0 lead that held up until halftime.

The Lancers stretched their margin to 13-0 on Roberts' three-yard run with five minutes left in the third quarter. It was a rugged 58-yard march [illegible] Jollymour's PAT kick [illegible] Lancers' scoring.

Up to that point, Pierce coach Jim Pendleton had been alternating sophomore quarterbacks Rick Maynard and Mike McCall, but he elected to switch to freshman Jeff Caprio, who immediately ignited the Brahmas' offense.

Completing five of five passes totaling 41 yards, Caprio drove Pierce 78 yards in only nine plays with Tim Brown getting the touchdown from one-yard out with two seconds gone in the final quarter. Pasadena aided the drive with 15 yards in penalties in the last 30 yards.

However, Pasadena's finest offensive moment was yet to come. With Caprio red-hot throwing completions all over the field and the momentum definitely in the Brahmas' favor, the Lancer defense came up with a brilliant stand to give PCC possession at its own 18. On third-and-one, Brooks Schiffman, Donna Nixon and Mitchell Pounds stacked up Tony Ervin for a yard loss and then Glenn Fletcher broke up Caprio's fourth-down pass intended for Margo Thornton at the five-yard line.

Moments later, the Lancer offense put together a six-minute, 30-second drive that killed any remaining hopes for the Brahmas.

Caprio ended with eight completions in 14 attempts for 126 yards to nearly steal the show from the Lancers. However, PCC's run-oriented attack took a page from Pierce's ball-control philosophy and won the ball game.

Pasadena CC [illegible]
Pierce [illegible]

[illegible]

TWO STARS—Don Roberts (right) and Reggie Brown are two of the leading Lancer rushers this season. Roberts led all the PCC backs in four of the five Metro games, gaining 613 yards overall. Brown was number one in the Pierce game, with [illegible] yards. [illegible]

Lancer twosome one of a kind

Brown, Roberts split time, honors

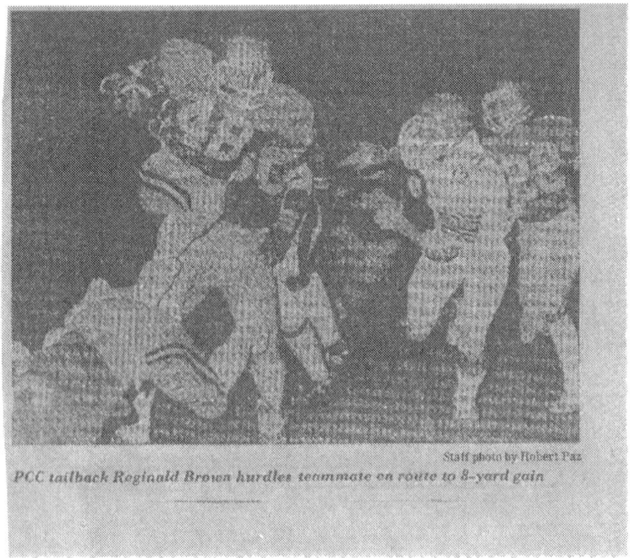

Staff photo by Robert Paz

PCC tailback Reginald Brown hurdles teammate en route to 8-yard gain

d Jackie Robinson's 10th Place

★ ★ ★ ★ ★ ★ ★ ★ ★ ★ ★

Reggie Brown Travels From New Jersey for Back and Football

By Brad Lehman
Sports Editor

He's called "Truck." When someone steps in front of him, he runs them over. If several defenders block his path, Truck steers away and accelerates. If the goal line is near, Truck just keeps on turning his wheels until he is into the end zone.

His Name is Reggie Brown.

Brown alternates at tailback with Don Roberts for the Lancers. Yet, even though he is only playing half of the time, he has 517 yards in just four games. And he wants more.

"Right now, I'm working on a 200-yard game," Brown said. "I want to do it before the season is over."

Brown also wants to gain 1000 yards on the season.

Passing Jackie Robinson for tenth place on the all-time PCC rushing list is another object Truck would like to achieve. Now, he is just about 11 yards short of the record.

"Every one (record) I can break I'll try. All I want to do is win. When I do crack it, I'll be happier. I want to make my name well known too."

Despite all his goals, sharing starting honors with Roberts does not bother Brown.

"When I'm in, I don't want to come out," Brown said. "It's between me and him to deal with is (sitting on the bench)."

Brown feels both he and Roberts have the same capabilities as running backs. There are not many things one back can do that the other cannot. But differences do exist.

"Donnie fakes well," Brown said. "If I could, I'd run around (defenders) more. "It seems like I use more power—it keeps me from getting too hurt. It just comes to me. 'Run into him, Reg.' If he comes at me, I want to hurt him before he hurts me.

"I'm glad I've got the size. I feel good with it. I feel I'm stronger. In the scrimmage (against Orange Coast) I got popped. I decided to put on weight. I put on a few pounds, and I feel better. I use mine (size) to my advantage."

Lately, though, Brown hasn't used his size as much to his advantage as he might have wanted. The defenders have been hurting him, rather than vice versa. Brown has two hip pointers, a bruised back, and he had a knot on his head from Fullerton.

"I have a different bruise every week. The hip pointers are painful. I go down and get treatment every day until I'm all right. Then I'm out taking care of business."

PUSHING THROUGH—Reggie Brown tries to push a Mt. SAC player's head off looking for more yardage. Lineman Dan Keesey watches the play from behind. Brown only rushed for 100 yards in 23 carries against the Mounties, his lowest total on the season. His total was reminiscent of the Lancers' play as they lost, 20-15.

Truck was injured more seriously two years ago.

"I came a long way. I hurt my back in high school. The doctor told me I'd never play a contact sport again. I was in the hospital. I was in traction. I had to wear a brace the last four games of the season, but I made it."

Brown "Came a long way" both figuratively and literally. He attended Malcolm X Shabazz High School in Newark, N.J. ("It was just a regular school.") Although he received an offer to attend Syracuse University with a full, four-year scholarship, Brown decided to come to PCC "to get away." His back has not hurt while out here either.

"I think it was the cold weather that caused the muscle spasms."

Hearing about PCC "through a chain of coaches," Brown started playing here last year. He led the Lancers to a Potato Bowl win last year over College of the Sequoias with four touchdowns.

"Every time I touch the ball I want to score. I just think about one thing—the goal line."

Brown stresses, though, he could not realize his constant will to score if not for his support up front.

"Without a line, ain't too much you can do. This is the best line I've ever been behind."

Another thing that helps, Brown said, is the crowd.

"When we have a full house, and everybody's cheering, ain't no way we can be denied."

Academically, Brown is concentrating on PCC and not wondering where he will be next year.

"I'm trying to take care of PCC. I am not saying where I'll be next, but I'm quite sure I'll be somewhere. My major is business administration-accounting. If I can take care of the books like I do the ball, it'll be great."

Without football, though, Truck would probably not be in school.

"School keeps me playing ball, and football keeps me in school. Football plays a big role in my life."

On and off the football field, Brown is interested in athletics.

"I'm a sports man," he said, motioning toward a football game on television. "I go out and party every now and then. I go bowling. There really isn't many things you can do during the season. During the week, you've got the books. Saturday's the game and Sunday there's the bruises."

With a little luck, Brown will be giving the bruises instead of taking them in the weeks to come.

Staff photo by Norm Denton

Reggie Brown (48) scores PCC's second TD off block by Dan Kessey (58)

4 [illegible] Los Angeles Times

TOP TAILBACKS—Pasadena City College tailbacks Don Roberts, left, and Reggie Brown practice for Saturday night's contest against Los Angeles City College at 7:30 at PCC.

Times photo by Joel P. Lugavere

PCC TAILBACK TANDEM ON THE RUN

Continued from First Page

[illegible] to six. He hasn't gained less than 100 yards in any game this year, and he is averaging nearly 6 yards a carry. He threw a pass for a touchdown against Mt. Sac and has caught five passes.

Roberts has not carried the ball as much, but has a slightly higher average, 6.3 yards a carry. Roberts also has caught five passes for 129 yards and two touchdowns.

At Temple City, Roberts' forte was running back punts and kickoffs, often for touchdowns. He spent his senior year breaking open games with long runs.

Roberts helped Temple City win CIF championships in 1976 and 1977, made the all-CIF team and was runner-up to Willie Gittens of Fountain Valley as player of the year in 1977.

Temple City coach Bob Hitchcock said, "He was the best high school football player offensively we ever had. I still can't understand why he wasn't recruited by major schools."

Roberts said he did not get any scholarship offers and rather than try to make a four-year team as a walk-on, enrolled at PCC.

Roberts, who is 5-11, 180 pounds, said he has the size and speed to play at a four-year school. Hyde agrees and said he is certain Roberts will also receive a scholarship [illegible]

[illegible] because of a strong offensive line and fullbacks Mike Sharp and Elijah Turner, has enabled Pasadena to develop the kind of ground game that opposing coaches call devastating.

Pasadena will play its final preconference game of the season when it hosts Los Angeles City College at 7:30 p.m. Saturday.

Fullerton, after losing what Hyde called the "game of the decade" in Pasadena last week, will play at Mt. San Antonio College at 1:30 p.m. Saturday.

Mt. Sac is 4-0 after defeating East Los Angeles last week, 28-12. This will be the first South Coast Conference game for both schools.

Mt. Sac coach Hal Exton said Fullerton, with quarterback David Wilson, is as strong in passing as PCC is in running.

"It's a key game for both of us," said Exton. "The winner gets a chance to go ahead and maybe win the conference."

In other community college games, Rio Hondo will play at 7:30 tonight at home against Harbor. Citrus will play at home at 7:30 p.m. Saturday against Southwestern, and East Los Angeles will play at home at 7:30 p.m. Saturday against Valley. Citrus opened the Mission Conference season with a 22-21 victory over Chaffey last week. Rio Hondo beat Grossmont, 31-24.

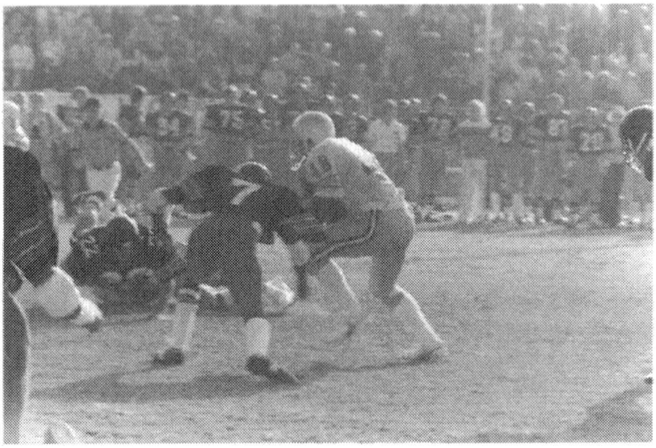

PCC played best game...

Continued from Page D-1

showed a nine-man front that caused the Lancers to "be outnumbered in the hole where we were running," but Hyde said his players "still went in there and threw their bodies at the nearest white jersey to make our running game go."

Hyde also mentioned the freshman players who played with "spirit and aggressiveness."

In all, Hyde summed up the Lancers' regular season-ending performance as a "very prideful one."

The victory also found perhaps the finest hours of tailbacks Reginald Brown and Don Roberts.

Brown, with 210 yards in 38 carries, became PCC's all-time rushing leader with 2,045 yards. He surpassed Sylvester Youngblood's 2,008 total gained in 1969-70.

"Sure, the record was in the back of my mind. It would have been impossible to keep something like that out," Brown admitted afterward. "But it wasn't foremost. Winning the game, earning the Metro championship and keeping alive the possibility of two more games were my first thoughts."

Roberts split time with Brown throughout the season and ranks No. 7 on the career rushing list with 1,545 yards. But with last week's loss of the club's top receiver, John Williams, to knee surgery, Roberts agreed to switch to wide receiver for the El Camino game and turned in a pair of sparkling catches, including a 43-yard touchdown strike from quarterback Mike Murray.

"If I have a choice, I would prefer to stay at tailback," said Roberts, who also was the hero of the last-second victory over Fullerton with a spectacular TD catch. "But the coaches asked me to go outside (flanker), that it would help the team, so what could I say? The team comes first."

PCC has two weeks before taking on the Valley Conference champion in a Dec. 1 post-season bowl game currently being called — for want of a better title — the Metro-Valley Bowl.

The Lancers' probable opponent is College of the Sequoias (in Visalia), although Fresno CC and Modesto still have chances for at least a share of the Valley title.

COS has been PCC's opponent — and the loser — in the last two Potato Bowls which matched the conference champions.

EL CAMINO-PCC STATISTICS

TEAM

Rushing

[illegible]

Passing

[illegible]

First downs

[illegible]

Total offense

[illegible]

Penalties

[illegible]

Fumbles-lost

[illegible]

INDIVIDUALS

Rushing

[illegible]

Passing

[illegible]

Receiving

[illegible]

Passing

[illegible]

Lancers Mash COS for Another Potato

PCC COURIER

SPORTS

Friday, December 8, 1978

Tailback Reginald "Truck" Brown en route to PCC career rushing record of 2,045 yards

...between blocks of Al Sanders (80) and Dan Keesey (58) in 34-3 win over El Camino that brought PCC's 3rd straight Metro title

Everyone did his job as PCC earns record title

By ROGER MURRAY
Executive Sports Editor

Saying he had never seen an El Camino College football team dominated in such fashion, Pasadena City College coach Harvey Hyde handed out praise for his entire team following its resounding 34-3 victory over the Warriors Saturday night that clinched for PCC its third straight Metropolitan Conference championship.

PCC, 8-2 and 4-1, became the first team to win three Metro football championships in a row. EC finished 5-5 and 2-3.

"Make no mistake, El Camino is a very good football team, with very good personnel," said Hyde after his club exploded for 27 points in the second and third quarters to keep alive its hopes for an invitation to the prestigious Dec. 8 Potato Bowl in Bakersfield.

"They are always a very physical team and this year is no different. But I felt we actually intimidated them from the second quarter on. Their quarterback (Don Morrow) took some hits I couldn't believe which had an effect on his concentration, and I don't think their receivers were as confident as they have been in other games this season."

Morrow entered the game as the Metro's top passer in terms of yardage (1,829) and touchdow[ns] (14), coming off an effort in which he completed [...] of 63 passes for 453 yards. El Camino also has fi[ve] of the conference's top 10 receivers statistically.

Hyde refused to single out individuals, preferri[ng] to cite groups for their performances that help[ed] the Lancers roll up 455 yards total offense and ho[ld] the pass-minded Warriors to 154, including a minu[s] 20 on the ground.

"It was probably our most complete game in a[ll] aspects," said Hyde. "I think we played our neare[st to] perfect football of the season."

Hyde praised place kicker Kambiz Ayria who n[ot] only drilled four conversions and field goals of [...] and 22 yards, but boomed his kickoffs in impressi[ve] style.

Hyde said the Lancers' punting (by Kerry Bur[...] and Jon Ryan) was the "best of the year and ga[ve] us good field position for the most part (wh[ich] penalties did not hurt the Lancers)."

The Lancer coach cited the PCC defense for [a] display of "aggressive, emotional football" and th[e] offense for playing with "reckless abandon."

El Camino's gambling defense often tim[...]

Turn to PC[...]
Page D[...]

***Interviewer*:** I bet people would be interested to know how you found out that you had made it into the pros. What was that day like?

Reggie: Whew, Draft Day, 1982. I'm at my fraternity brother's house. Me and all my Kappa brothers and a bunch of other friends were hanging out watching the draft.

So you know the 1st round went by, ugh. 2nd round went by. I was like "are you serious man, nothing yet"? 3rd round went by, I got up and went home. I was upset because I just knew that somewhere in there I was going to get drafted.

So I just laid down and all of a sudden the phone rang. It was Leeman Bennett from the Atlanta Falcons. He said Reggie Brown, how'd you like to come down and play for the Falcons? I said YES!!!

I couldn't control the excitement!

1549	2272	50000
College career rushing yards	PCC all-time leading rusher title	Audiences reached US & abroad

FRESHMAN YR	277 yds 4 TDs	Potato Bowl
COLLEGE CAREER	1549 yds 16 TDs	Pasadena
1ST YR PRO	scored winning TD	Against the Vikings
PRO CAREER	played 7 yrs	Atlanta Falcons and Tampa Bay Buccaneers
FINAL YRS	played 2 yrs USFL	Retired w/ Philadelphia Eagles

It’s like it happened yesterday and I tell you it was like the biggest thing that ever happened to me until that point in my life. It really was so big for me.

Remember, I was the guy in high school when I hurt my back they said I couldn’t play any more sports for the rest of my life … so when I look back on all that I accomplished during my college years, it’s even more gratifying. Many of the records that I set still stand today.

I was honored to have been inducted into the Pasadena City College 2015-2016 Hall of Fame as the school's all-time Leading Rusher. It was one of my best accomplishments to return to the school nearly 20 years later to be acknowledged and express my gratitude in return.

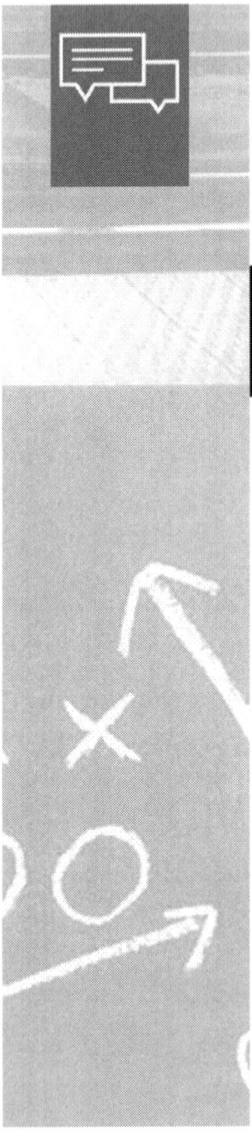

CREATE YOUR OWN PLAYBOOK.

What skills do you have or need to learn to help create the new opportunities?

Skills that I already have:

Example: using social media, creating Facebook or Instagram accounts, finding useful apps, taking photos or creating video with my phone

New skills that I want to learn:

3RD
QUARTER

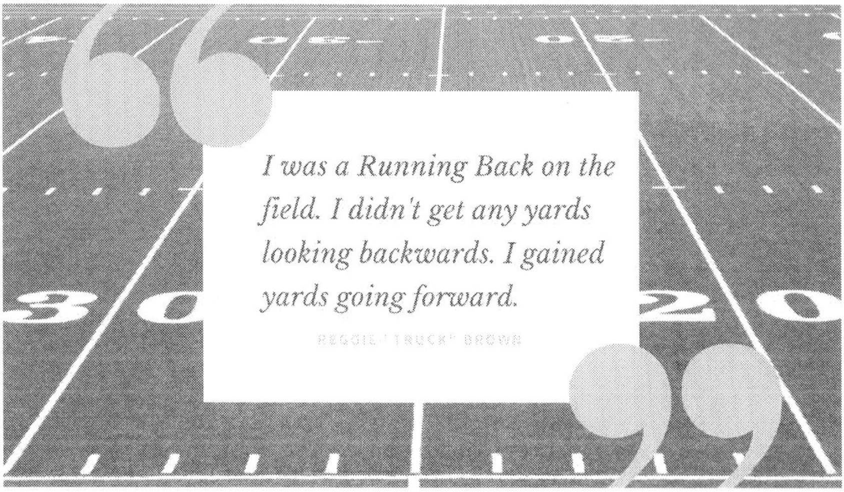
I was a Running Back on the field. I didn't get any yards looking backwards. I gained yards going forward.
REGGIE "TRUCK" BROWN

Interviewer: Now it's 3rd quarter and you made it to the NFL. Most people think it's all glitz and glamour. Walk us through the real journey.

Reggie: Well, you're in the NFL. People think you're making a whole bunch of money and you living like a king. But no one ever thinks about what really goes on behind the scenes.

Interviewer: So let's talk about the pros and the downfall. Let's get to that, because the name of the book is "*What Happened to the Playbook?*" and the struggles that you had to endure when you no longer had a playbook.

Reggie: Ok, I'm going to go back to Atlanta -- playing with the Falcons. It was a great time and you're this hero, and everybody wanted to be around you. Everybody wanted to have a good time with you.

> *My best time was when I got drafted by the Atlanta Falcons.*

It was the absolute best time I ever had in my life. I left Newark heading off to college to make something of myself so when I made the team, things were going great!

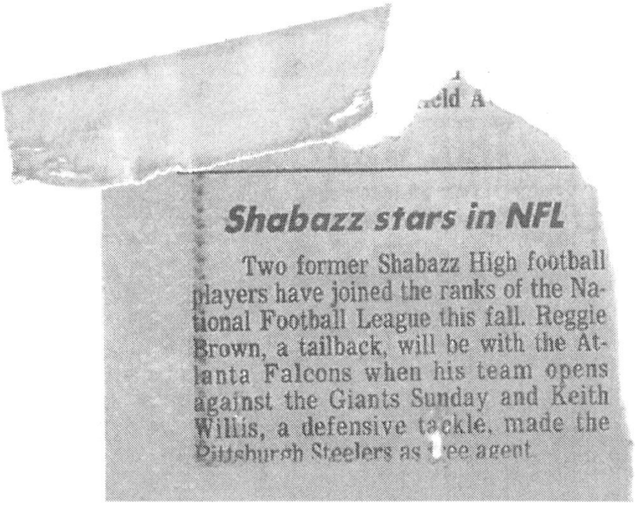

Shabazz stars in NFL

Two former Shabazz High football players have joined the ranks of the National Football League this fall. Reggie Brown, a tailback, will be with the Atlanta Falcons when his team opens against the Giants Sunday and Keith Willis, a defensive tackle, made the Pittsburgh Steelers as free agent.

But things happen. And they're not always in your control. The year I got drafted is the same year we had an NFL strike, so we didn't play a whole full season. Things happened that got in the way so I wasn't really getting the money that I was supposed to get.

Then the next year, we had a coaching change. So the coach came in, cleaned house, and I was one of those unfortunates who got released by the team.

> *It was such drastic thing getting cut on my 24th birthday. I didn't know whether to cut the cake or cut my wrists.*

So from the Atlanta Falcons, I went on to the USFL and went to play with the LA Express. Steve Young got a contract for $50 million and I got a contract worth $50 thousand. I didn't get to figure out how that worked so I complained, and they released me.

Going forward from the 1984 season to 1985, I went on to play with the Arizona Outlaws in the USFL with Doug Williams as Quarterback and we had a chance to play against the LA Express that same year.

So here I am going against a team that released me the year before.

I had 185 yards, scored 3 touchdowns and the game was on national TV on a Monday night!

I loved it and had a great time.

Talk about peaks and valleys. I tell you, man this was the valley experience.

That year ended with the Outlaws and the following year the USFL went to court against the NFL. They won the contract, but they only got three dollars. So the league folded ... I moved on again.

This time to the Tampa Bay Buccaneers. Just so happened that I injured my foot during the last preseason game against the Miami Dolphins and they released me.

But, according to the agreement the team wasn't really supposed to release players while they're injured, so after speaking up I ended up getting paid for that year, but it seems that I was blackballed. I really just did what I felt that I needed to do.

So here I am back to square one again. I came home back to New Jersey and pouted in my room for about a month. Lo and behold, I received a call with a shot to play for the Arizona Rattlers who had recently merged with the Oklahoma Outlaws. I was back in the game…

Then as fate would have it in 1987, I got the awesome chance to play with the Philadelphia Eagles. But as life would have it, turned out to be yet another strike year.

By this time the game just wasn't fun anymore, so I decided that I was going to retire and that's just what I did.

I retired as a Philadelphia Eagle.

24

***Interviewer*:** With all of those changes, different cities, different franchises, different leadership, how did you adjust to all of the ups and downs?

***Reggie*:** Well one thing I did understand and that's why I left the league when I did – it was business. It's big business. When you don't do your part, they find someone else to do it.

If you don't like the way they're doing something, then you go somewhere else. Trust me … I could say a lot of different things about the business side of football but that's not the name of the game.

At the end of the day, I got an opportunity to play and that's more than most. I had a good time while I was doing it, I retired – fairly healthy. But now all these years later, my body hurts. My body really does hurt.

When I think back, it was just before I retired when the pain started to set in. You know, I get a little injury here, a little injury there. Then the trainer would give me the pain meds to get through the game.

Matter of fact I remember one game in particular. We played the San Francisco 49ers and lost.

I got some serious bumps and bruises. So I get on the plane and this time they give me the pain meds with half a six pack.

> *By the time we got 20,000 feet in the air, I was higher than the plane.*

I remember starting to do things trying to find more drugs and alcohol to numb the pain. By now, it seemed like I was in pain after every single game and it continued that way until I left the game.

Problem is after I was out of the football scene I was still feeling pain. What was I going to do to make the pain go away now? And where would I get it from?

***Interviewer*:** Ok, you're not playing anymore, still in pain and I guess at this point you're heading back to New Jersey. What's life in Newark looking like?

***Reggie*:** You know, I can say Newark is a great place to be from but I can't say it's a great place to go. I got all these friends, and they're happy to see me.

It's like I was a hero when I first got back. Everyone wanted to hang out. But I was really no different than anybody else. I just played professional football for a while.

Not all, but there were lots of people who wanted to be around because they thought I had some money. By now, alcohol and drugs were everywhere and it all really started to take over my life. I just found myself doing the same things over and over again.

I started asking myself lots of questions. What am I doing? How did I get to this place?

Football is over. The money is running out and there's no more playbook. I'm like man, now what?

The money started running low so for a while I was working as a truck driver to make ends meet. I enjoyed being on the road and things were going okay. But eventually I had to check in to a program to deal with the drugs and alcohol that had consumed me. The program did help to a point but before long, I was right back to doing the same old things.

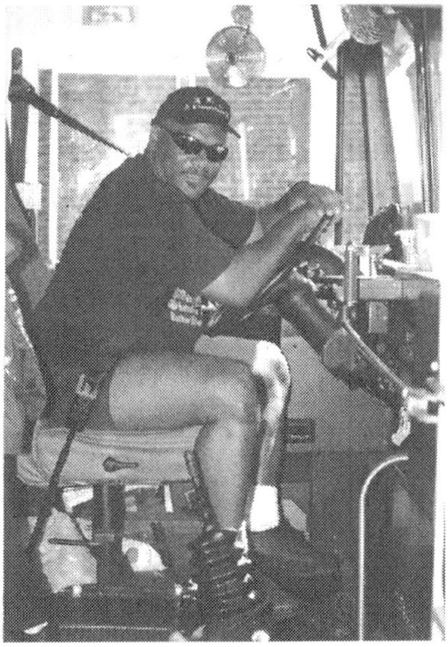

I really just went ahead and took the program and used some of the things I learned for a little while I was there. But the moment I got out of the program, all the stuff was still there waiting for me. It didn't change.

> *I was going to have to change but I didn't know how to do that.*

Even to this day, I struggle with certain things in my life but I don't have to do the same things that I used to do because I realized that I needed help. It was really serious and I was suffering so much but no one really knew it.

Sometimes you hear people say they lost their family. **I will say that I didn't lose my family. I gave up my family**. I lost them in the process of my struggles, with pain, with loss, with addiction, all of my ups and downs.

Today, my children are my greatest sense of pride. I always say that my son taught me how to be a father and when my daughter was born, she taught me how to be a man.

Interviewer: It seems this is the REAL reason why you wanted to write this book.

Reggie: You know, I needed to write this book. My struggles and poor choices were so real for so long and I truly just had no idea how to fix them. People don't see the deep-down nitty-gritty about what you have to do to make it out here, then how hard and long you fight to claw your way out of the hole once you're in it.

When you're faced with a decision, stop & ask yourself ... Do I want to have "a good night" or " a good life"?

I did more drugs than a whole lot of people. But no one ever saw that. Even if they did, they wouldn't have said anything because after all I'm Reggie Brown, pro football player. Back then, you couldn't tell me anything.

But I really needed help in the worst way.

They say, "no pain no gain." Well there's lots of pain in my personal playbook. It's not just my life either. There are so many ball players and professional athletes in this boat. Of course, not every ball player goes through it.

But I was one of those who did.

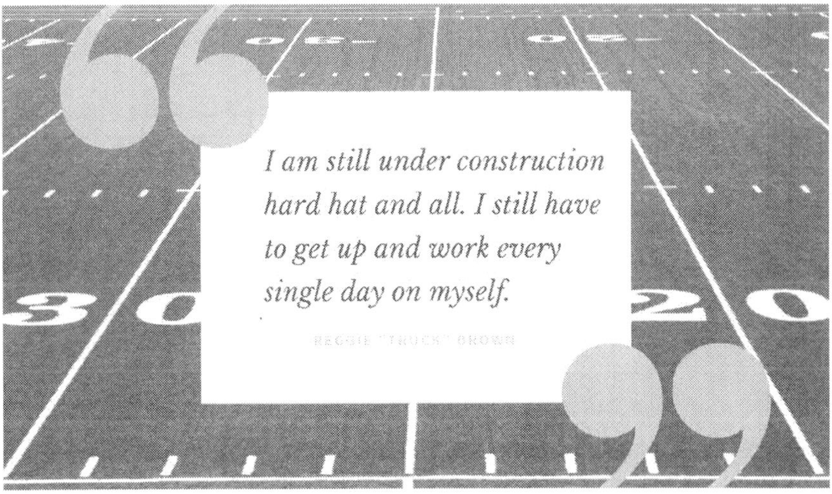
I am still under construction hard hat and all. I still have to get up and work every single day on myself.
REGGIE "TRUCK" BROWN

CREATE YOUR OWN PLAYBOOK.

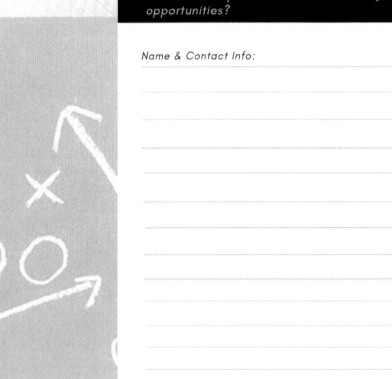

Who do I know or would I like to meet that could help me create new opportunities?

Name & Contact Info:

4TH
QUARTER

***Interviewer*:** So, the third quarter was all about the Pros. Now we're winding down. What's the 4th Quarter?

***Reggie*:** 4th Quarter is life after football. You know NFL means "Not For Long". After my final season was over and I turned in the playbook I had lots of questions for myself.

How do I adjust to life after football? What do I do now? Do I just go get a job – be a regular guy. You know football players are not really regular people. Life after football is so different. Trying to even explain it now and put it into words is hard. It's real life I had to deal with and real situations.

There are some things I know how to handle. What I can't handle, I get on my knees and I say "okay Lord help me out" and here I am today doing the best I can. Consistently persistent is what I like to say. That's me, I don't give up very easily.

***Interviewer*:** You mentioned the business of football and you're an entrepreneur now and have run your own business for a long time. Do you feel like any of those years as an athlete helped prepare you for the business world?

***Reggie*:** Absolutely. One of the things about entrepreneurship and sports. It taught me about never giving up. You know sometimes you get into things that don't work out too well and you say oh I don't want to do it anymore and you quit – too early.

But just another week, another day, another hour could have been the difference between you making it all the way and you not making it at all.

***Interviewer*:** You want to talk about some of things that you have going on now that it's after the game. I know you're doing some work with your fraternity.

You're going to be doing some more work with young people. Why don't you talk about your work in the community.

Reggie: Well since I can remember way back when, I was always involved in the community I was living in. Because when I was coming up, if someone came in to talk to us and they had been to a place where you were trying to get to, you want to sit down and listen to them.

Today I find that there's so much that I must give back. The only way that I can keep what I have is to give it away.

To me, it's an opportunity. It's not always about money. It's not always about someone knowing who you are, it's just about giving back. There's so much work to be done.

We talk about it takes a village to raise a child. I ask people well when are you going to get started in your village?

There are villages all over the place waiting for someone to come in and say "hey, I have a hand to lend … what do you need"?

I tell you whenever you see a bunch of kids or youth, I guarantee you'll see me right there because that's what I enjoy doing.

Interviewer: Is that what prompted you to transition into your motivational speaking with your business "Great Day to be Alive"?

Reggie: Someone told me that if you do something for 30 days, it becomes a habit. So can you imagine me getting up every day complaining -- it's raining, it's snowing. It's cold outside, it's hot outside. Ugh.

Listen, it doesn't matter whether it's raining, hailing, sleeting, or snowing, it's another great day. That's all I know. It doesn't change for me. There's never a bad day. If your day isn't going well then just stop … and start all over again.

RBP
REGGIE BROWN PRODUCTIONS
ATHLETE SPEAKER
ENTREPRENEUR
GREATDAYTOBEALIVE.NET

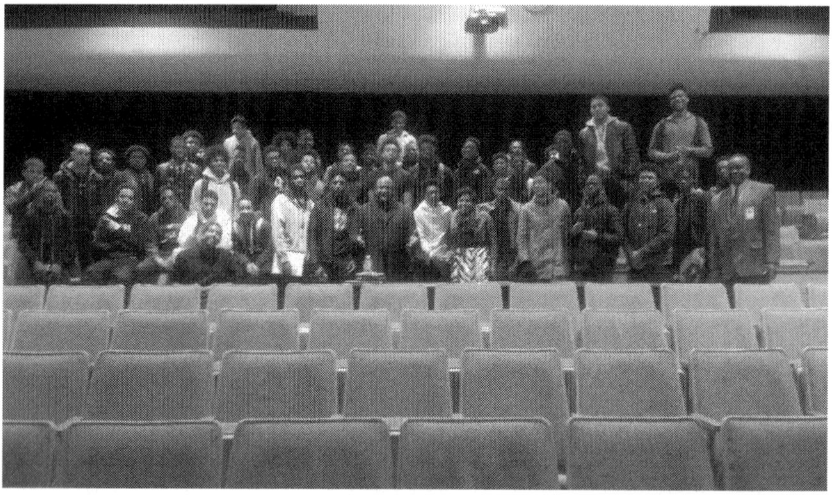

Beyond
Expectation

Beyond
Screening

Beyond
Expectations
film & tv.

Look angelic.

Motivational and Transitional Speaker
" Every day you wake up is truly a great day to be alive! "
Having fun
Helping people
Makin' money
- Reggie Brown

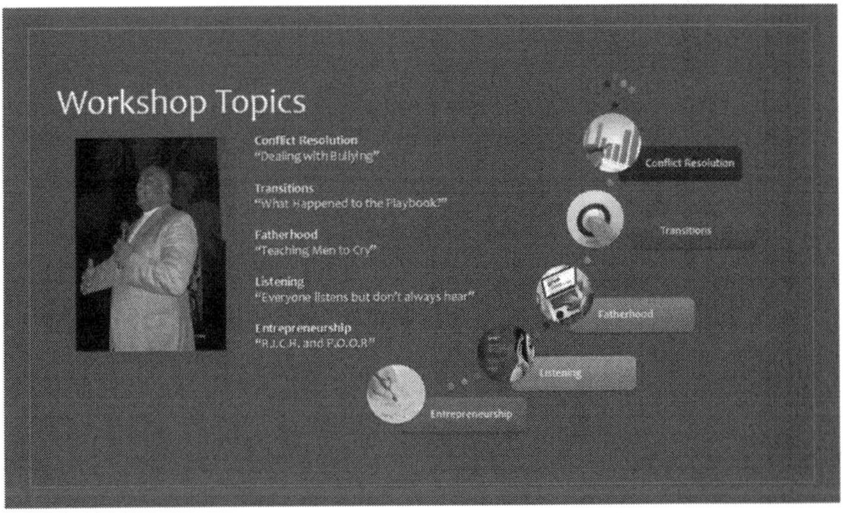
Workshop Topics
Conflict Resolution
"Dealing with Bullying"
Transitions
"What Happened to the Playbook?"
Fatherhood
"Teaching Men to Cry"
Listening
"Everyone listens but don't always hear"
Entrepreneurship
"R.I.C.H. and P.O.O.R"
Conflict Resolution
Transitions
Fatherhood
Listening
Entrepreneurship

POST
GAME

REGGIE BROWN, CEO
Reggie "Truck" Brown, former running back with the Atlanta Falcons, Tampa Bay Buccaneers, and the Philadelphia Eagles, is a highly sought after speaker for corporate conferences and community events.

PASADENA CITY COLLEGE HALL OF FAME

"Our next inductee stands as PCC's all-time leading rusher for 2,272 yards. He played on back to back Metropolitan Lancer football teams in 1978 and 1979. An All-American, he led PCC to 2 college titles including the Potato Bowl when he rushed for a PCC record 277 yards and scored 4 touchdowns.

His 1,549 rushing yards in 1979 stayed a school record for 22 years and his 257 attempts that season remains a Lancer's record.

After earning a scholarship and playing at the University of Oregon he was drafted #95 in the 4th round of the 1982 NFL draft by the Atlanta Falcons.

In 1985 he rushed for more than 1,000 yards and led the team in touchdowns for the USFL's Arizona Outlaws. He returned to the NFL to finish his pro career at Philadelphia in 1987.

Please welcome to the podium 2016 Hall of Fame Inductee Reggie Brown!"

"I want to thank Pasadena and the coach that allowed me to come here from New Jersey in 1978. You see I was that guy that they said wasn't good enough to go to a major college because my grades weren't good enough. I had 1.99 GPA coming out of high school, so I had to go somewhere.

A coach that I played with in New Jersey knew one of the coaches here. They connected and sent some film and I left New Jersey in 1978 with a one-way ticket, $50 and a suitcase and I said I'm not coming back until I do something with my life or making something of myself.

20 years later, I'm back.

It was such an honor to be here and play with the teams that I played with. I had a bad back in high school. They said I couldn't play any more sports for the rest of my life. That means baseball, football, hockey, soccer, track. You name it.

They said I couldn't do it. That's what the doctor said. But one thing -- they forgot to ask me!

You control your own destiny. When I got here, I was #7 on the depth chart so I didn't think I was going to play anytime soon but I just wanted to know what I was supposed to be doing. Guys started getting hurt and they said, "put that guy in". All I wanted was an opportunity.

I'm from Newark NJ – Malcolm X Shabazz High School. Bad back. They said I wouldn't make it. None of that mattered to me because I was here playing football. I didn't go to school to get an education. I went to school to play football.

I'm gonna' be real with you. The best thing that ever happened to me was East Colorado Boulevard. I was like man, I'm somewhere I can do something with my life. Whole lot different than what it was in New Jersey. You know people see things, but they don't see what it can be. But if you change the way you look at things, the things you look at will change. So, you know what? I started looking at life a little differently.

Today, I'm sitting here listening to the introduction about what I've done. Listen, all I know is the coach said give him the ball 38, 39 toss. All I did was run.

I'm from New Jersey, that's all I did was run. So, they let me do something I enjoy doing. What did I have to lose?

Today, all I do now is help people, have fun, and make money. All I want to do is help somebody and what I stand for is HOPE. Helping Other People Everywhere. That's all I do.

I came from Philadelphia, Pennsylvania a couple of days ago. They cancelled my flight because it was about to be blizzard, but I got on an earlier flight because I had to get here. You see, I'm never on time but I'm never late. Hear me now, cause I'm always early. I didn't want to miss this.

This is an opportunity for me to say thank you Pasadena for allowing me to come and share a bit of what I had with you. This guy over here, Coach Hyde. That was my guy. He said give him the ball. Keep giving it to him. 257 times I'll take it. You got some more coach? I'm ready to go!

Thank you so very much. I could say so much more ... but God bless, see you at the top."

REGGIE BROWN #24
FOOTBALL
MORE THAN FOOTBALL
ENTREPRENEUR
FATHER
MOTIVATIONAL SPEAKER &
CEO
GREAT DAY TO BE ALIVE
2015-16
PASADENA CITY COLLEGE ALL-TIME LEADING RUSHER
REGGIE "truck" BROWN
HALL OF FAME
Reggie Brown (1978-79, Football)
PCC's all-time leading rusher for a career at 2,272 yards, Brown played on back-to-back Metropolitan Conference champion Lancers teams in 1978 and 1979. He played on two Bowl champions, including the Potato Bowl title victory over College of the Sequoias in '78 when he rushed for a PCC bowl record 277 yards on 35 carries and scored four touchdowns.
After earning a scholarship and playing at the University of Oregon, Brown was drafted No. 95 overall in the fourth round of the 1982 NFL Draft by the Atlanta Falcons. Brown played parts of three seasons in the NFL, finishing as a running back for Philadelphia in 1987.
PCC head coaches:
Eric Widmark, Harvey Hyde

Interviewer: That's so great that you were inducted into the PCC Hall of Fame. Before we wrap up, let's please talk about what you're up to today.

Reggie: I'm a motivational/transitional speaker. The reason why I say transitional is sometimes when you motivate, you have to keep motivating. When you transition to the next level, it goes a little bit deeper.

Interviewer: From what I've read, you're now a highly sought-after speaker for corporate events and conferences all across the country. How did you get into this type of business?

Reggie: When I retired from playing football people used to ask me to come and speak quite a bit. I like to talk so I kind of enjoyed it.

At one particular event, a pastor asked me to come and have lunch with a speaker who was onsite, and he asked me one question – what's your best ability? I said flexibility, durability. He said "no, it's availability" and at that point I knew this was something that I wanted to do. Make myself available to others. It's an awesome experience when you can do what you feel like you were called to do.

Interviewer: It sounds like you want to reach more people. Students or adults or both?

Reggie: I actually speak with both on a number of topics. One of my most requested is around these two words RICH and POOR. You know what RICH says? - Realizing It Can Happen. How about POOR? Passing Over Opportunities Repeatedly.

You have opportunities before you right now than you can believe with access to more information today than we've ever had … so it's up to you to decide "which life do I really want to lead?"

Interviewer: Looking back on everything now, do you have any final thoughts or tips that you would share from lessons you've learned?

Reggie: You know, if I had to sum it up I would say that today I make better choices - starting from the moment that I wake up in the morning. Here's just a few…

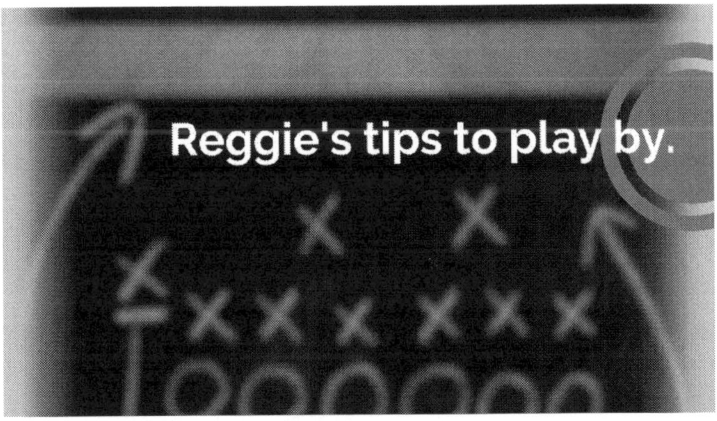

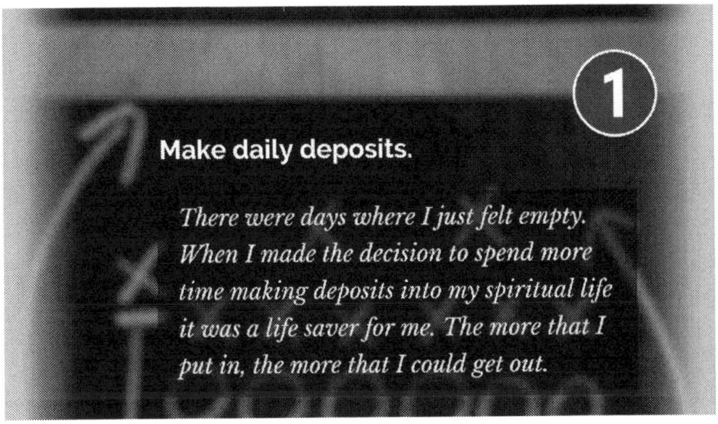
1
Make daily deposits.
There were days where I just felt empty. When I made the decision to spend more time making deposits into my spiritual life it was a life saver for me. The more that I put in, the more that I could get out.

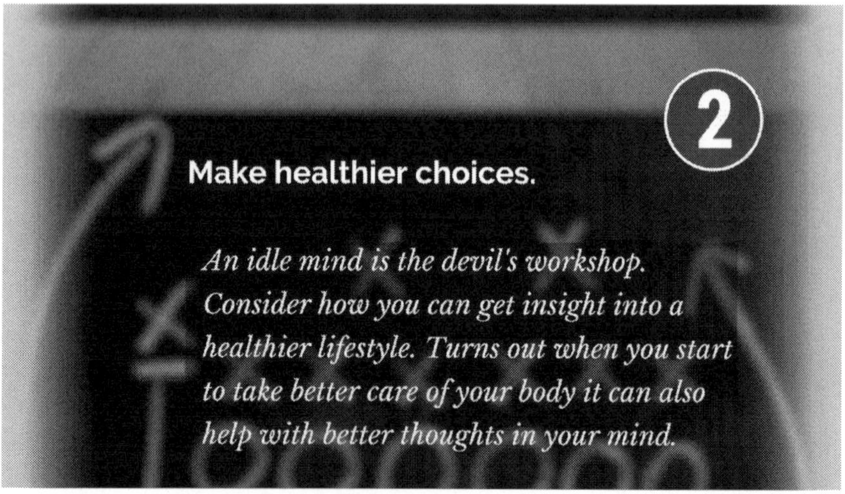

2
Make healthier choices.
An idle mind is the devil's workshop. Consider how you can get insight into a healthier lifestyle. Turns out when you start to take better care of your body it can also help with better thoughts in your mind.

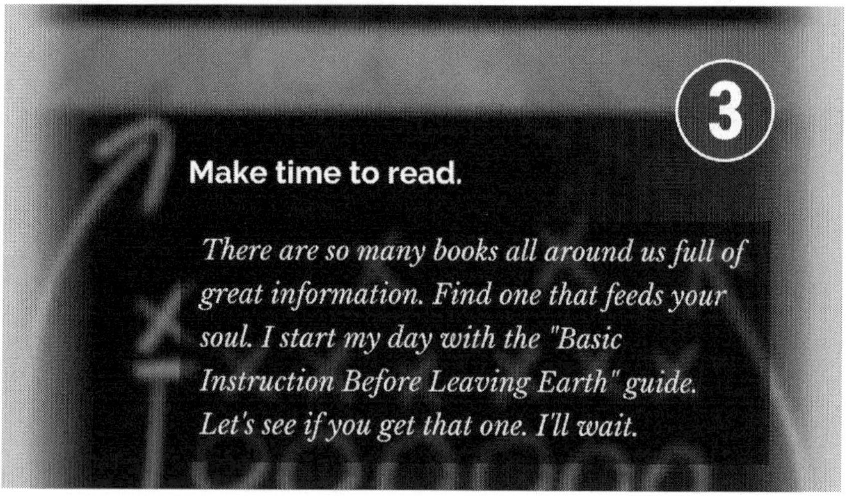

3
Make time to read.
There are so many books all around us full of great information. Find one that feeds your soul. I start my day with the "Basic Instruction Before Leaving Earth" guide. Let's see if you get that one. I'll wait.

I definitely have more to share from my personal experiences. It's these life lessons plus other requested topics like Sportsmanship, Mentorship, Entrepreneurship (and more) that I enjoy sharing when I go out and speak to people … whether young or old.

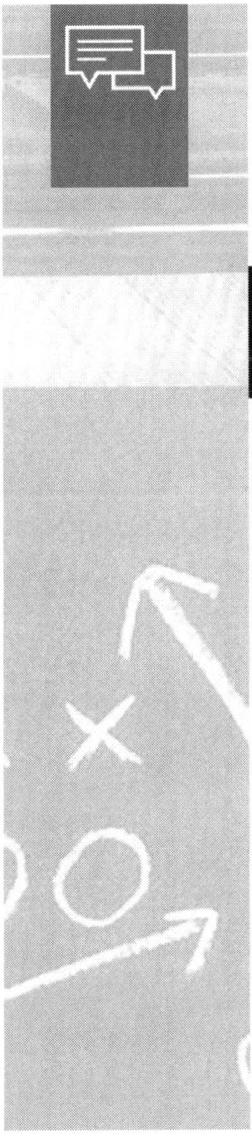

CREATE YOUR OWN PLAYBOOK.

Sportsmanship. Develop a positive mental attitude.

- [ ] *Read books, articles or watch videos that can help me with positive professional development.*
- [ ] *Search for information written by or created by professionals who have created success.*
- [ ] *Find and follow writers in your area of interest in publications like Forbes, Inc., Success Magazine, Entrepreneur Magazine, Black Enterprise*

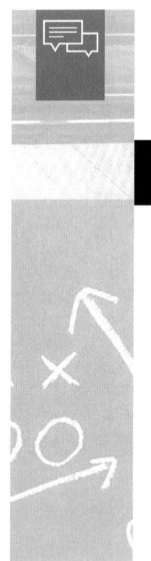

CREATE YOUR OWN PLAYBOOK.

Mentorship. Seek out mentors that are where you want to be professionally.

- [ ] *Identify professional(s) that I want to meet. Invite them to a "Cup of Coffee" for 15-20 minutes of their time.*
- [ ] *Consider church pastors, relatives, local store owners, coaches, doctors, professional organizations.*
- [ ] *Attend local business events, high school or college alumni events and think about opportunities to volunteer to help meet new professionals.*

CREATE YOUR OWN PLAYBOOK.

Entrepreneurship. Start to develop an employer vs. employee mindset.

- [ ] *Consider every skill that I have that could be a potential opportunity to make my own money and attend networking events. Go alone or bring a friend.*
- [ ] *List new skills that I can learn online or attend a class. The more that I can do = the more $ that I can make.*
- [ ] *Think about a 'Plan B' based on those skills if sports or professional athlete is my initial career goal.*

I'll leave you with this... **Do you have dreams and goals for your life but some days you're just not quite sure how you'll ever get there?** You've read my story. I knew early on that I wanted to play pro ball, but I wasn't sure exactly how I would make it. I just started to put in the work and decided to get myself on the right path. I got hit upside my head lot so I'm crazier than most and I don't deny it.

I've had more than my share of bumps, bruises, bad choices and mistakes making my way from the streets of Newark to the NFL.

Yes, I was down and out for more than a minute. I lost just about everything that I had and ever loved. I didn't appreciate it at the time. The road back was hard, ugly, and long, really long. But one thing happened along the way that I hadn't expected.

It was the people – the genuine people who showed up at different times in my life who really cared about me and helped me make it through and get to where I am.

All these years later, many of those people are still in my life today. Believe me when I tell you that I'm thankful for each and every one of them because when I think back on it, I really can't tell you what else I would have done or where I would have ended up if not for football.

I still struggle at times with things but what keeps me going is my faith, my beautiful family, and knowing for a fact that there are some streets to this very day that I can't drive down because they would lead to my definite end.

So if you've ever wondered why I always say that every single day you're blessed to wake up is truly a "Great Day to be Alive!!!" … now you know why.

Love you much,

Reggie

Welcome
Eagles
Legends

BOOK
NOW
KEYNOTE SPEAKER
APPEARANCES
AUTOGRAPHS

ABOUT THE AUTHOR

Reggie "Truck" Brown is a professional athlete, speaker, and entrepreneur. He played 7 years in the National Football League with the Atlanta Falcons, Tampa Bay Buccaneers, and retired with the Philadelphia Eagles in 1987.

As a featured Motivational/Transitional speaker and CEO of Reggie Brown Productions, he has addressed audiences of more than 50,000 people across the United States and abroad since his days in the pro football league.

More information and bookings >> www.greatdaytobealive.net

49487153R00062

Made in the USA
Columbia, SC
23 January 2019